Doughnuts

Victoria Blakemore

For Kendyl, thank you for sharing your sweet idea!

© 2019 Victoria Blakemore

All rights reserved. This book or parts thereof may not be reproduced in any form, stored in any retrieval system, or transmitted in any form by any means—electronic, mechanical, photocopy, recording, or otherwise—without prior written permission of the publisher, except as provided by United States of America copyright law. For permission requests, write to the publisher, at "Attention: Permissions Coordinator," at the address below.

vblakemore.author@gmail.com

Copyright info/picture credits

Cover, LittlePigPower/Shutterstock; Page 3, LittlePigPower/Shutterstock; Page 5, Yuliia Kononenko/Shutterstock; Page 7, Barbara Delgado/Shutterstock; Page 9, Aimee M Lee/Shutterstock; Page 11, Greatstockimages/AdobeStock; Page 13, Africa Studio/AdobeStock; Page 15, JUNESAMA/Shutterstock; Page 17, Jason Vandehey/Shutterstock; Page 19, Brent Hofacker/Shutterstock; Page 21, Elena Zajchikova/Shutterstock; Page 23; fahrwasser/AdobeStock; Page 25, arinahabich/AdobeStock; Page 27, Rawpixel.com/Shutterstock; Page 29, Cheangchai/AdobeStock; Page 31, Anastasia Turshina/AdobeStock; Page 33, Aquarius Studio/Shutterstock

Table of Contents

What are Doughnuts?	2
Ingredients	4
Yeast Doughnuts	6
Cake Doughnuts	8
History	10
Making Doughnuts	14
Fillings	18
Doughnut Holes	20
Doughnuts and Other Food	22
Doughnuts Around the World	24
Nutrition	26
Doughnut Festivals	28
Recipes	30
Glossary	34

What Are Doughnuts?

Doughnuts are sweet treats that are made by frying or baking balls of dough. They are also called "donuts."

There are two main kinds of doughnuts, yeast doughnuts and cake doughnuts. They differ in ingredients, taste, and **texture**.

There are many **varieties** of doughnuts. The can be made with different fillings, toppings, icings, and glazes.

Ingredients

Most doughnuts are made with flour, sugar, eggs, milk, vanilla, oil, and salt. Many recipes also call for oil to fry the doughnuts in.

They also need something to make the dough rise as it cooks. Some are made with yeast. Others are made with baking powder or baking soda.

Many other **pastries** are made with the same ingredients. They differ in the **quantities** and how they are prepared.

Yeast Doughnuts

Yeast doughnuts are made with yeast in the dough. Yeast is actually a living **fungi**. It breaks down sugars and makes dough rise when it is baked.

Yeast doughnuts are not very sweet on their own. They need a glaze or sugar coating to be sweet.

Yeast doughnuts are lighter and fluffier than doughnuts made without yeast. They are also more chewy.

Cake Doughnuts

Cake doughnuts are made without yeast. They rise when they are baked because they are made with baking soda or baking powder.

Cake doughnuts can be baked or fried. Some are made in doughnut pans. Others are **piped** into a doughnut shape.

Cake doughnuts are thicker and more solid than yeast doughnuts. They are also heavier than yeast doughnuts.

History

Different **cultures** have been eating fried dough for thousands of years. The food that is closest to the doughnut first came from the Netherlands.

Olykoeks were made by Dutch **immigrants** when they came to America in the 1800's.

Olykoeks were balls of dough fried in oil or fat. The center didn't cook as fast as the outside, so they were often filled with fruit or nuts.

A ship captain named Hansen Gregory is thought to have made doughnuts with holes in the center. When he cut out the center, the doughnuts cooked more **evenly**.

In 1920, the first **automated** doughnut machine was created by Adolph Levitt. It was shown at the World's Fair in 1934.

Now doughnuts are sold in stores and markets all over the world.

Making Doughnuts

Yeast doughnuts are made a special way in factories and bakeries. First, the ingredients are measured and mixed in large mixers.

The dough is **kneaded** and left to rest so that it can rise. Once the dough has risen, it is ready to be shaped and fried.

Doughnuts can be fried in a deep fryer or in a large pot. There are also machines that drop dough into large fryers to cook.

Doughnuts are often shaped by a special machine called an extruder. It cuts the dough into circles and cuts a hole in the center.

Then the doughnuts are given time to rise again. Once they have risen, they are fried in hot oil. Last, they are ready to be iced, glazed, or filled.

In factories and some bakeries, doughnuts move along a track. They go under a stream of glaze. It coats the top, sides, and part of the bottom with a sweet glaze.

Filled Doughnuts

Filled doughnuts do not have the center cut out. Instead, their center is filled with jelly, cream, or other fillings.

In factories, filled doughnuts are cut into circles and fried. Once they are fried, they move into a special machine that **injects** the filling into the center.

Filled doughnuts can also be iced or glazed. They are often covered with powered sugar.

Doughnut Holes

Doughnut holes may have been first made by a ship captain in Maine. It is said that he was tired of the uncooked centers, so he cut out the middle.

Doughnut holes are made by cutting a circle in the doughnut dough. The dough balls are then fried.

Doughnut holes are often covered in powdered sugar or a sweet glaze after they are fried.

Doughnuts and Other Food

Some people add doughnuts to other food to create fun new recipes.

Doughnuts are often added to sweet desserts. They can be used as the buns for ice cream sandwiches. The dough can also be cooked in a waffle iron to make doughnut waffles.

Some restaurants use doughnuts as buns for burgers or sandwiches.

Doughnuts Around the World

Fried dough treats are made all over the world. In Italy, they make bombolonis. The dough is fried in a ball and filled with a cream or custard.

In South Africa, they make koeksisters. The dough is braided, fried, and soaked in a syrup. They are sticky and sweet.

It is a Jewish tradition to make sufganiyahs during Hanukkah. These **pastries** are fried and filled with a fruit jelly.

Nutrition

Doughnuts are high in calories, sugar, and fat. They are very low in protein, so most of their calories come from sugar and fat.

Doughnuts contain calcium, folate, and vitamin K. These **nutrients** are good for your body, but there are healthier ways to get them than eating doughnuts.

Doughnuts are not the healthiest of treats. They should be eaten in **moderation.**

Doughnut Festivals

Doughnut festivals are held in many different countries. At these festivals, people can do and try lots of different kinds of doughnuts.

Festivals are a fun way to see and taste many new and fun kinds of doughnuts. Many festivals also have music and shows.

Doughnut stands in street markets are also good places to find fun doughnut treats.

Recipes

Easy Baked Doughnuts

Makes 9 doughnuts

Ingredients:

1 cup sour cream   2 eggs

1 1/2 tsp vanilla extract   1 cup sugar

2 cups flour   1 tsp baking soda

1/2 tsp salt   1/2 cup vegetable oil

Directions:

1. Preheat oven to 350 degrees Fahrenheit. Grease doughnut pan.

2. Mix sour cream, oil, vanilla, eggs, and sugar in a bowl.

3. Stir in baking soda, flour, and salt. Mix well.

4. Pour batter into pastry bag or plastic bag with cut corner

5. Squeeze batter into doughnut pan, filling each cavity 2/3 full.

6. Bake until golden brown, 12-15 minutes. Remove from oven and cool on wire rack.

Doughnut Glaze

Ingredients:

1 1/2 cup powdered sugar

4 Tbs milk   1/2 tsp vanilla extract

Food coloring (optional)

Directions:

1. Mix all ingredients in a wide bowl.

2. Dip doughnuts halfway in, covering the tops

3. If desired, add additional toppings (sprinkles, colored sugar, chocolate chips, etc.)

Glossary

Automated: something that is done by a machine without human help

Cultures: the language, customs, and ideas of a group of people

Evenly: equally, the same all the way through

Fungi: living things that are similar to plants, but cannot make their own food like plants do

Immigrants: people who move from one country to another

Inject: to force a filling into the middle of a doughnut

Moderation: not having too much

Nutrient: something in food that helps people to grow

Olykoeks: "oily cakes," balls of fried dough made by the Dutch

Pastries: sweet baked goods

Piped: when dough is squeezed out of a pastry bag to make shapes

Quantities: amounts

Texture: the look and feel of something

Varieties: kinds

About the Author

Victoria Blakemore is a first grade teacher in Southwest Florida with a passion for reading.

You can visit her at

www.elementaryexplorers.com

Also in This Series

Also in This Series

www.ingramcontent.com/pod-product-compliance
Lightning Source LLC
Chambersburg PA
CBHW041321110526
44591CB00021B/2870